I0882531

This pattern is all about the preparation, with much of the work done to individual components before final assembly. That makes this a great project to do in stages. (Of course, if you're impatient like me, you can stitch it all in one sitting.) Once you have the weaving finished, the pockets added to the lining and outside pieces, the straps sewn and trimmed, the buckles placed, and so forth, sewing the backpack together is amazingly quick!

I've given instructions for a few different material options. The main backpack as shown has a woven kraft•tex front. The Greenery and White Charlie backpack has a heavy (eleven-ounce) denim for the other outer material. The Blue Iris and Blue Turquoise Charlie backpack has a lighter-weight (seven-ounce) denim. The Radiant Orchid and Stone Charlie backpack uses suiting-weight fabric. If you are using quilting-weight cottons, I've included instructions for additional interfacing to stiffen things up. If you're using pleather (one of my favorite materials for bags of all kinds!), I've given instructions that eliminate seam allowances on the straps and so forth.

As a bag maker, the single resource that improved my abilities and my final results more than anything else was reading Nicole Mallalieu's book *The Better Bag Maker* (by C&T Publishing). What a revelation! I encourage you to check it out.

MATERIALS

Yardage includes enough for the wristlet as well as the backpack.

kraft•tex 1: 1 roll

kraft•tex 2: 1 roll

Front fabric (use only if not weaving with kraft•tex): ½ yard or 1 fat quarter

Back fabric: ⅞ yard

Lining fabric: 1⅛ yards

Fusible interfacing (midweight to stiff): 3 yards (I use Pellon 931TD.) (When using a lightweight fabric for the back, increase to 3½ yards.)

CUTTING

NOTE

For a solid front instead of a woven one, cut 1 piece 16½″ × 17½″ for the front.

Front fabric

kraft•tex 1

- Cut 2 strips ½″ × 27″ for weaving.
- Cut 4 strips ½″ × 25″ for weaving.
- Cut 4 strips ½″ × 22″ for weaving.
- Cut 16 strips ½″ × 20″ for weaving.
- Cut 4 strips ½″ × 19″ for weaving.
- Cut 4 strips ½″ × 15″ for weaving.
- Cut 4 strips ½″ × 12″ for weaving.
- Cut 4 strips ½″ × 9″ for weaving.
- Cut 4 strips ½″ × 5½″ for weaving.

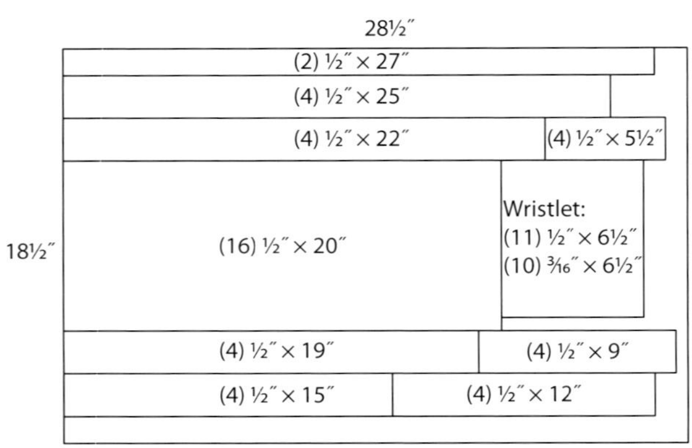

Fusible fleece (use only if your exterior is pleather): 3″ × 28″

Base material, such as plastic canvas: 8½″ × 10⅛″

12″ zipper: 1 for top opening

7″ zippers: 3 (1 for exterior pocket, 1 for interior pocket, 1 for wristlet)

Purse feet: 4

1″ buckles: 2

Small swivel hook: 1

Eyelets: 10 (with eyelet setter)

kraft•tex 2

- Cut 14 strips 1″ × 18½″ for weaving.
- Cut 1 piece 8″ × 1½″ for the lining zipper-pocket frame.

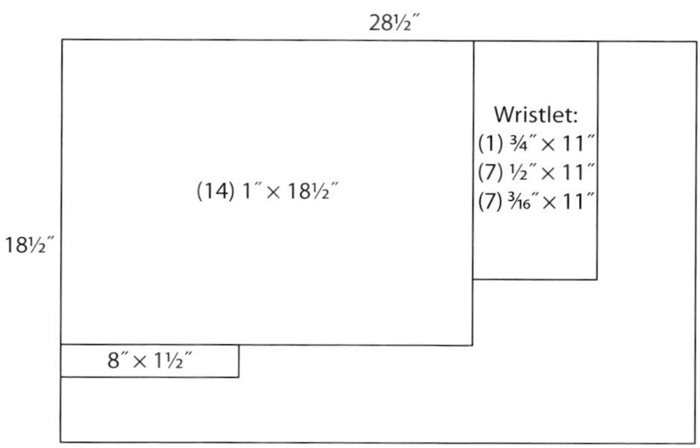

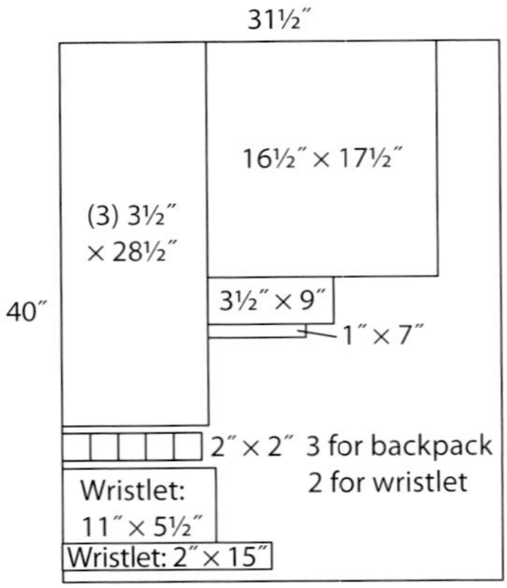

Back fabric

- Cut 1 piece 16½″ × 17½″ for the back.
- Cut 3 strips 3½″ × 28½″ for the straps. (When using pleather, cut 6 strips 1″ × 28″.)
- Cut 1 piece 3½″ × 9″ for the strap anchor. (When using pleather, cut 1 piece 1″ × 9″.)
- Cut 2 squares 2″ × 2″ for the zipper tabs. (When using pleather, cut 2 rectangles 1½″ × 2″. When using denim, cut them from lining fabric *or* cut 2 strips ½″ × 2″ from kraft•tex.)
- Cut 1 square 2″ × 2″ for the key-hook strap. (When using heavy denim, cut 1 rectangle 1″ × 2″.)
- Cut 1 strip 1″ × 7″ for the strap bands. (When using pleather, cut 1 strip ⅜″ × 7″.)

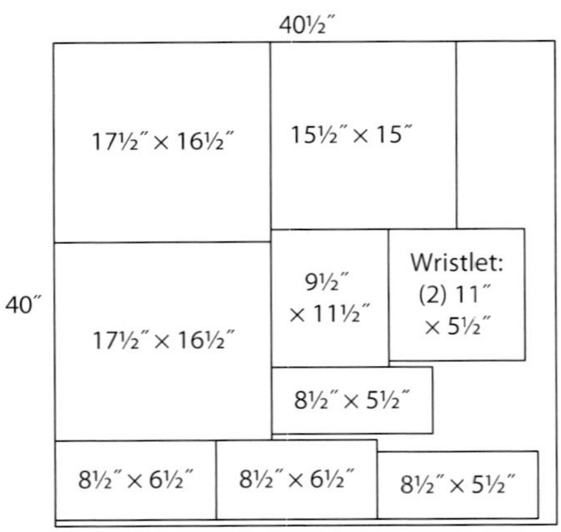

Lining fabric

- Cut 2 pieces 17½″ × 16½″ for the front and back lining.
- Cut 2 pieces 8½″ × 5½″ for the zipper pockets.
- Cut 2 pieces 8½″ × 6½″ for the zipper pockets.
- Cut 1 piece 15½″ × 15″ for the compartment pocket.
- Cut 1 piece 9½″ × 11½″ for the base wrap. (*Optional:* Use scrap fabric instead of lining fabric for this piece.)

Interfacing

- Cut 4 pieces 16½″ × 17½″ for the fronts and backs. (When using a lightweight fabric for the back, double your interfacing by cutting 5 pieces.)
- Cut 2 pieces 8½″ × 6½″ for the zipper pockets.
- Cut 2 pieces 8½″ × 5½″ for the zipper pockets.
- Cut 1 piece 15½″ × 7″ for the compartment pocket.
- Cut 3 strips 3½″ × 28½″ for the straps. (Strap interfacing is not necessary if your fabric is heavy denim.)

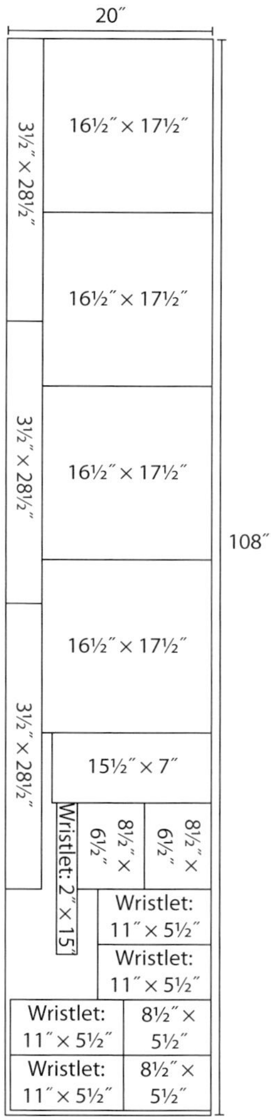

Fusible fleece

- When using pleather for the straps, cut 3 strips ⅞″ × 28″.

Base material

- Cut 2 rectangles 4¼″ × 10⅛″.

Tools and Notes

This bag uses a variety of purse findings and sewing notions such as buckles, zippers, eyelets, purse feet, and swivel hooks. It's also constructed with kraft•tex, which has its own minor stitching challenges. The backpack can definitely be sewn using your standard tools and supplies. That said, I find that adding a few different tools really makes it easier to construct.

Sewing feet: I am constantly switching between my edge-stitch, zipper, and open-toe foot. With the edge-stitch foot, the edgestitching on the woven kraft•tex strips is so fast and easy! (I actually use my blind-hem foot instead of investing in a designated edge-stitch foot.)

Glue and staples (*Staples?*): Because you can't pin through kraft•tex without leaving holes, I recommend glue tacking the pieces together. I prefer Fabri-Tac because it instantly holds the pieces together. Be very careful not to let the glue press out onto the visible sections; it is permanent glue. You can use tacky water-soluble glue, if you prefer, or binder clips where possible.

If I've used a heavyweight fabric like denim, I will use staples to baste the front, back, and bottom together when stitching the boxed corners on the outsides. Once the seam is sewn, I remove the staples.

Hole cutter: When setting the eyelets in the straps, you will need to cut through four layers of fabric and interfacing. My eyelet hardware came with a heavy-duty hole cutter. On heavier fabrics where I can't make the hole cutter work, I end up using small, sharp-pointed scissors to nip away at the little circles. Patience is needed, but it works every time.

Sewing with kraft•tex: When stitching kraft•tex, use a sharp needle and lengthen the stitches. (I use length 3 on a BERNINA.)

Weaving

1. Edgestitch both long edges on the 1″ kraft•tex 2 strips and set aside.

2. Using the weave template as a guide, lay out 8 of the 20″ kraft•tex 1 strips on the vertical strip 1 lines.

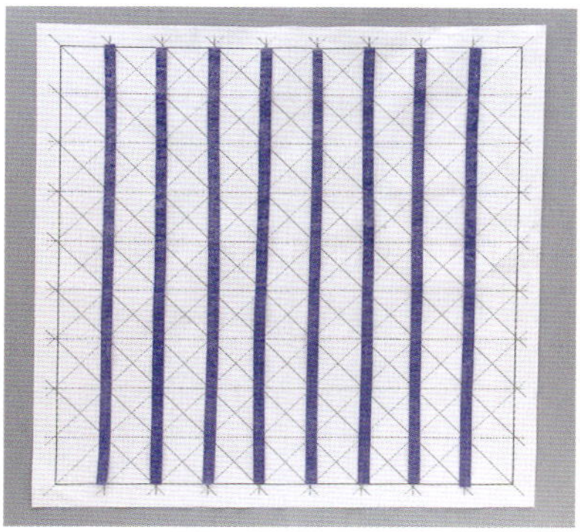

3. Lay out 8 of the 20″ kraft•tex 1 strips along the horizontal strip 2 lines. As you go, use double-sided tape or glue to tack the strips together at the intersections. (I use 2 long rulers placed on top of the vertical strips to hold them in place as I go.)

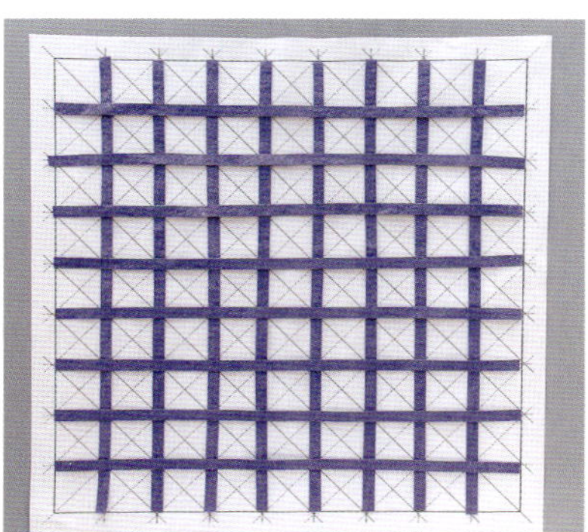

4. Sew a line down the center of each strip in the grid. *Do not sew the strips to the grid.* Take only the kraft•tex strips to the sewing machine.

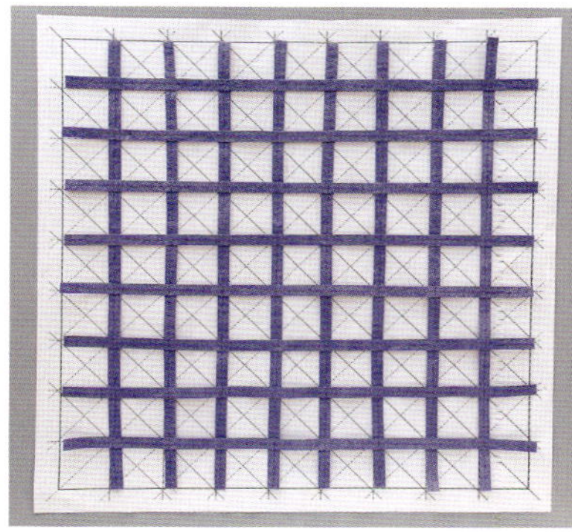

5. Lay a 27″-long strip along the diagonal strip 3 line, going from corner to corner. Work outward, and reduce the length of the strips as you go. (The 25″ strips are on either side of the 27″ strip, followed by the 22″ strips, and so on. The 5½″ strips are in the corners.) As you go, use double-sided tape or glue to tack the strips to the grid at the intersections.

6. Sew a line down the center of each strip 3 diagonal strip.

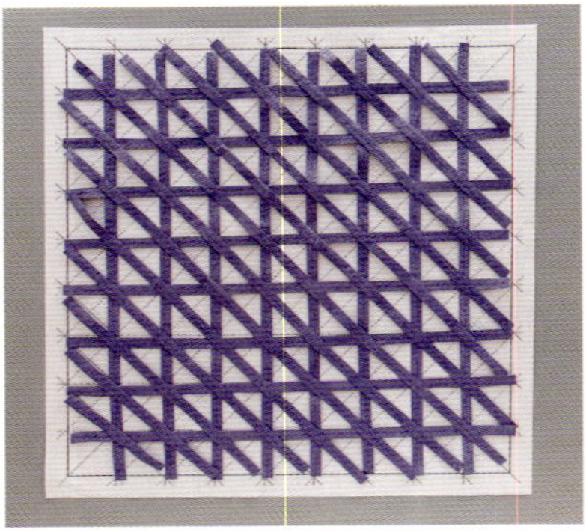

7. Repeat Steps 5 and 6 to lay out and sew the strip 4 diagonal strips.

8. Weave 7 of the 1″ kraft•tex 2 strips horizontally across the sewn grid, going under the strip 1 strips and over the intersections.

9. Weave 7 of the 1″ strips vertically down the grid, going under the horizontal kraft•tex 1 strips and over the intersections and also weaving on top of and below the horizontal 1″ kraft•tex 2 strips.

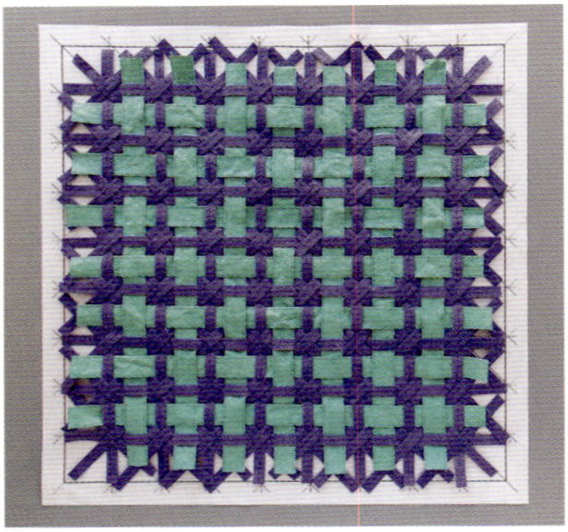

10. Fuse the 16½″ × 17½″ interfacing on the back side of the woven panel, carefully centering on a vertical strip.

11. Place the Charlie kraft•tex Backpack front and back pattern on top of the grid, and center on a vertical 1″ strip. (You will have a little wiggle room top to bottom.) On the finished bag, the top seam along the zipper will be ¼″–⅜″. It's best to keep the edges of a kraft•tex strip away from that seamline. Once you are satisfied with the placement, mark the cutting lines.

12. Stitch ⅛″ in from the marked cut line.

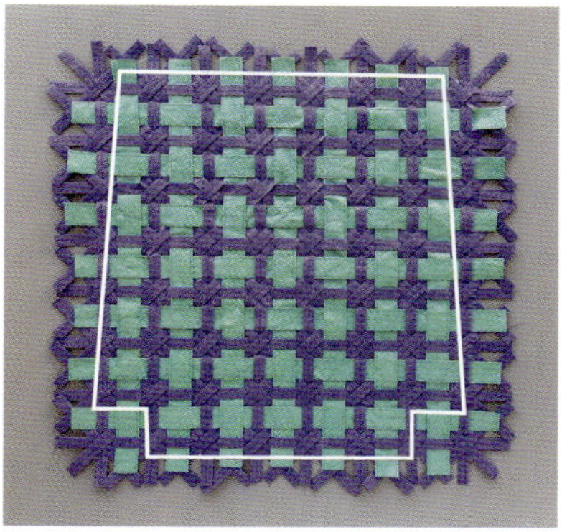

13. Cut out the front along the marked lines.

Construction

Use ½″ seams unless otherwise noted.

Prepare the Fronts and Backs

1. Prepare your front and back paper pattern. I cut out the rectangles for the outside front zipper pocket and the lining zipper pocket. I added all positioning marks by punching small holes at the circle marks for the purse feet placement, the 2 inside corners of the buckle strap placement, and the 4 corners of the kraft•tex zipper-pocket frame (10 marks total). I notched the edges at the triangles for the compartment pocket placement and the buckle strap placement (8 notches total).

2. Fuse interfacing to the outside back and the lining front and back pieces. When using a solid front instead of a woven front, include it in this process.

3. Use the front and back pattern to cut out the outside back and the lining front and back pieces.

4. Use the pattern and an erasable marker or chalk to mark the zipper pocket placement on the outside front, the buckle strap placement on the outside back, and the purse feet placement on both front and back. If you are weaving your front, move the zipper placement to work best with your weave. Use the pattern to mark the compartment pocket placement on the lining front. Use the pattern to also mark the lining zipper-pocket placement and the 4 corners of the kraft•tex zipper-pocket frame on the lining back.

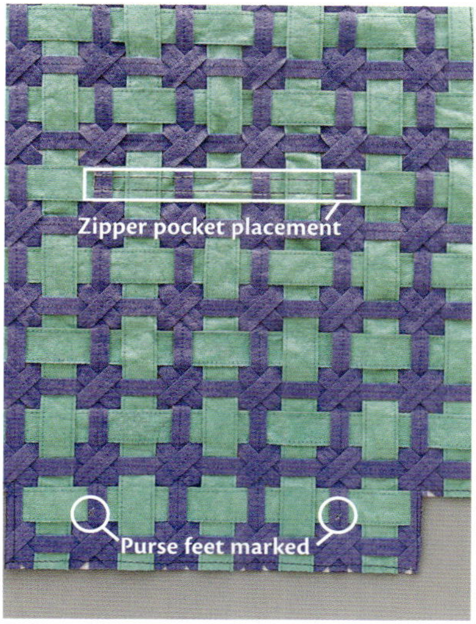
Zipper pocket placement
Purse feet marked

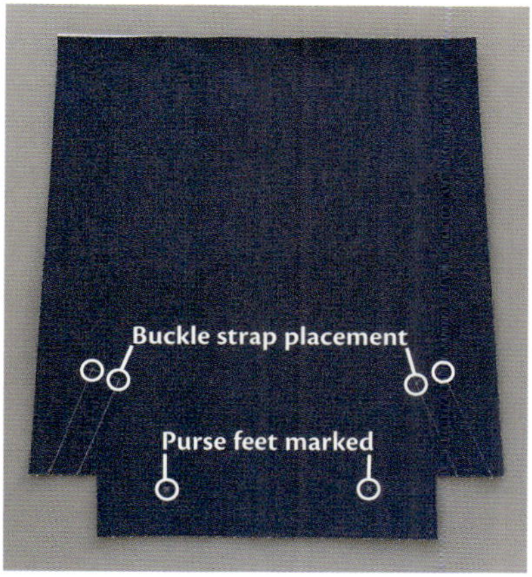
Buckle strap placement
Purse feet marked

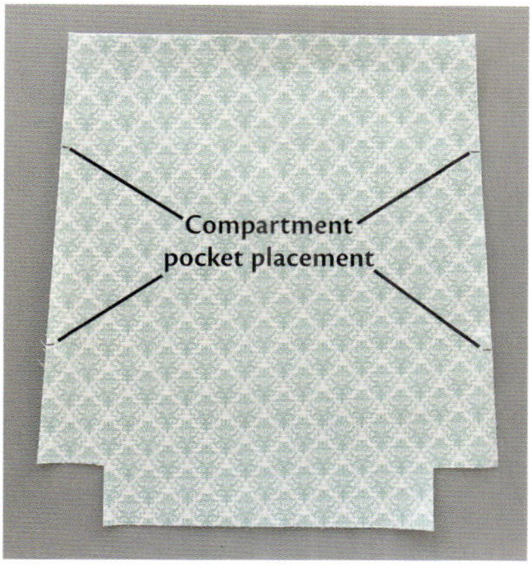
Compartment pocket placement

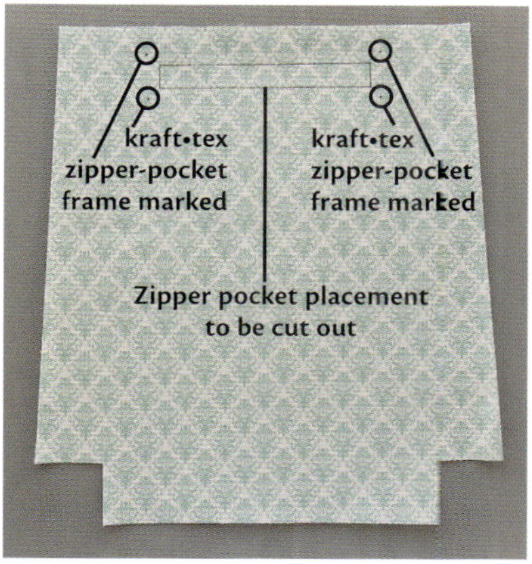
kraft•tex zipper-pocket frame marked
kraft•tex zipper-pocket frame marked
Zipper pocket placement to be cut out

Create the Straps

The strap pieces to be prepped are the shoulder straps, the strap anchor, the handle strap, the strap bands, the buckle straps, and the key-hook strap. If you are using quilting-weight cotton or other light- to medium-weight fabric, fuse the interfacing to the wrong side of the strap pieces before Step 1.

When using heavy denim, you'll have a 1″ × 2″ key-hook strap instead of a 2″ × 2″ strap. In Step 2, fold the two edges toward the center.

When using pleather, fuse a ⅞″ strip of fusible fleece to the center of 3 strips 1″ × 28″. Place the fused strips, wrong sides together, with the nonfused strips, and tack together with glue. Topstitch the edges and ends of each strap.

1. Fold one end of a 3½″ × 28½″ strap in ½″ and press. Repeat with another one of the remaining straps. On the last strap and on the 3½″ × 9″ anchor piece, press under both ends.

2. Fold a 3½″ × 28½″ strap in half along the length. Press. Reopen and fold both edges toward the middle to create a 1″ × 28½″ strap. Repeat with both of the remaining straps, the strap anchor, the 1″ × 7″ strap band, and the 2″ × 2″ key-hook strap. Set the strap anchor piece aside.

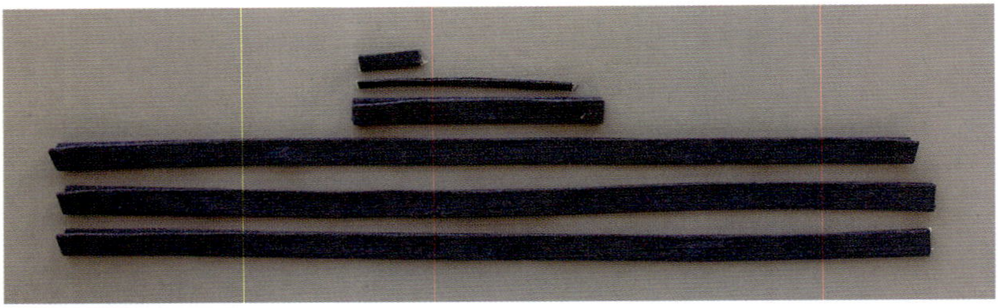

From top to bottom: Key-hook strap, strap band, strap anchor, two shoulder straps, one long strap (used to make two buckle straps, one hand strap)

3. On the 2 long straps that have one end folded in, topstitch along the long edges and across the folded-under edge. On the strap that has both ends folded under and on the key-hook strap, topstitch just along the long edges. On the narrow strap band, topstitch down the middle along the length. Set aside the strap band piece and the key-hook strap.

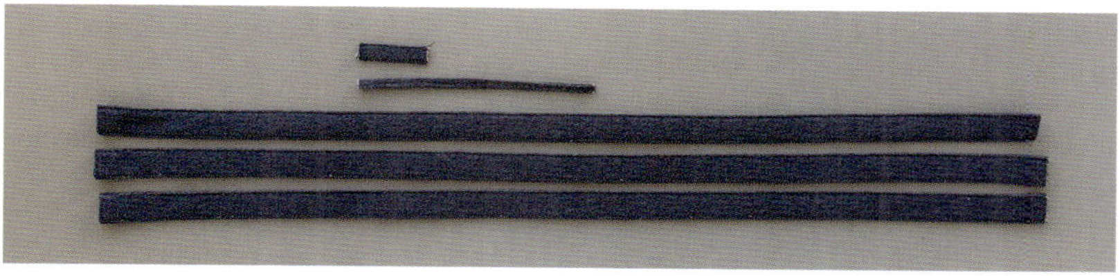

4. On the long strap that has both ends folded under, cut 2 pieces 8″ long from the ends for the 2 buckle straps. Cut a piece 10″ long for the handle strap. Set aside. *Fig. A*

5. Mark the eyelet placement on the folded-under ends of the 2 remaining long straps (these are your 2 shoulder straps). Mark in the center of the strip: 1″ from the folded-under end and then 3 other marks, each 1½″ apart (at 1″, 2½″, 4″, and 5½″ from the end). *Fig. B*

6. Use the instructions on your eyelet setter to create the 8 eyelets. *Fig. C*

A From top to bottom: two buckle straps, handle strap

B

C

Make the Buckle Straps

1. Cut in half the narrow strap band piece you set aside in Create the Straps, Step 3. You will have 2 strap bands that measure ¼″ × 3½″. (The strap bands are used to hold the loose end of your straps in place.) *Fig. A*

2. Create a loop with each 3½″-long strip, overlapping the ends ½″. Take a few stitching lines on the overlap to secure. Set these strap bands aside. *Fig. B*

3. On the folded-under end of the buckle straps, mark the position of the hole for the buckle prong: 3″ from the folded-in end and centered (½″ from each edge). *Fig. C*

4. Using your eyelet setter, insert an eyelet at the mark. (If you do not wish to use an eyelet here, you can just cut a small hole.) *Fig. D*

A

B

C

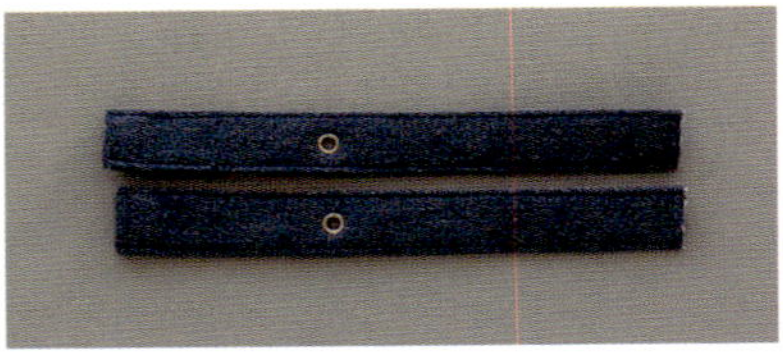

D

5. Feed the buckle prong through the hole from the back, and fold the remaining 3″ of the buckle strap to the back. ***Fig. E***

6. Feed a strap band onto a buckle strap so that the band sits 1″ below the buckle. The overlap should be on the back and should be covered by the finished buckle strap end.

7. Topstitch the folded-under end of the buckle strap in place across the end, anchoring the strap to itself. Topstitch near the buckle, locking the strap band in between the stitching lines. ***Fig. F***

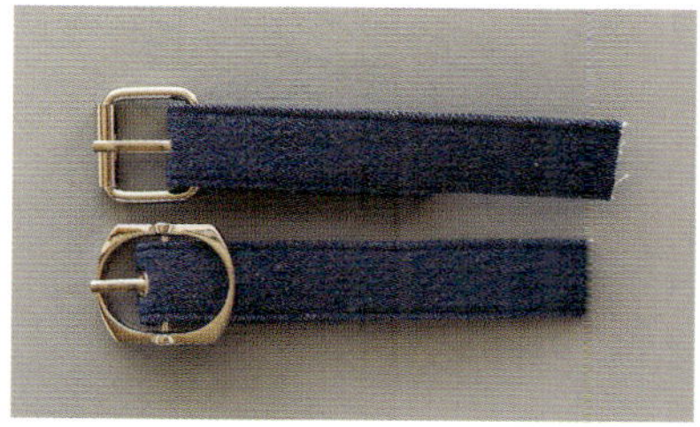

E Either style of buckle will work.

F

8. Use the placement marks on the pattern to position the buckle strap to the outside back piece—wrong side of the strap to the right side of the back. The unfinished end will extend past the edge of the back. Tack the strap in place ¼″ from the edge.

Construct the Strap Anchor

1. Use the strap anchor placement guide to mark the strap placement lines on the inside of the strap anchor you set aside in Create the Straps, Step 2 (page 14).

2. Working with the long open edge of the strap facing up, pin or glue the unfinished end of a shoulder strap in place. (The 2 outer marks are for the shoulder straps.) The raw end should be within 1⁄16″ of the fold so it will be caught in the topstitching. The right side of the shoulder strap should be facing up (wrong side of the strap toward the work surface).

3. Repeat Step 2 for the remaining shoulder strap at the other end of the strap anchor.

4. Pin or glue the handle strap in place using the 2 center strap marks on the anchor piece. Make sure not to twist the handle as you place it.

5. Pin or glue the strap anchor closed, encasing the strap ends.

6. The side of the strap anchor that is currently facing up is the wrong side of the strap anchor. Position the strap anchor on the outside back piece, 1¼″ from the top and centered side to side, with the wrong side of the strap anchor facing down onto the right side of the back. All of the straps should be coming out of the top of the anchor.

7. Topstitch around all 4 sides of the strap anchor.

Attach the Purse Feet

The brad-style purse feet have two prongs attached to the foot that fold over a circle-shaped back.

1. Center a circle-shaped back that came with the purse feet over one of the purse-feet marks. Use the 2 parallel cutouts in the circle back to mark the cut-out lines on the bag front or back.

2. Use a sharp tool to cut along those slits. ***Fig. A***

A

3. Feed the prongs of the purse foot through those slits from front to back. Slide the circle back onto the tabs, and press the tabs away from each other to secure the purse foot in place. (*Note:* If your fabric is lightweight, cut 1″ × 1″ squares of interfacing or scrap fabric. Cut slits in them, too, and slip those over the prongs between your purse fabric and the circle back to give your feet more to hold onto.)

4. Repeat Steps 1–3 with the 3 other purse feet.

Make the Base

1. Center the base material on top of the 9½″ × 11½″ base wrap fabric.

2. Fold the fabric around the base and tack. I fuse using ½″ fusible tape or glue tack in place. Leave the ends loose.

3. Set aside.

Create a Lining Compartment Pocket

1. Fuse the 15½″ × 7″ piece of interfacing to the back of the 15½″ × 15″ compartment pocket piece, ½″ from one long edge. *Fig. A*

2. Fold the pocket in half lengthwise, right sides together (15½″ × 7½″), and sew along the open long edge.

3. Turn right side out and press with the seam on one long edge.

4. Topstitch along the folded edge. *Fig. B*

5. Fold the pocket in half and crease to mark the vertical center.

6. Using the compartment pocket placement guide on the Charlie kraft•tex Backpack front and back pattern, place the pocket right side up on the right side of one lining piece.

7. Topstitch along the bottom of the pocket and stitch up the creased centerline to create 2 compartments.

8. Line up the edges of the pocket with the edges of the lining and pin in place. This will create fullness in the pockets.

9. Baste along the edge with a ¼″ seam. *Fig. C*

A

B

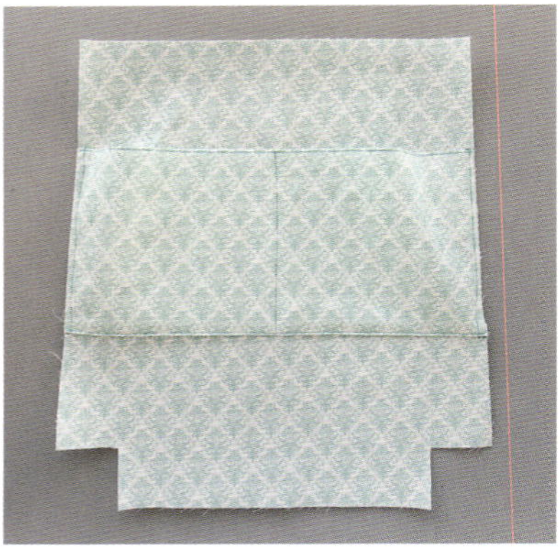

C

Make the Zipper Pockets

If you are using zippers longer than 7″, you will need to shorten them (see Shortening a Zipper, page 26).

1. Fuse the zipper pocket interfacings to the wrong side of the zipper pocket pieces.

2. Place a zipper on top of a 8½″ × 6½″ pocket piece, right side of the fabric to the wrong side of the tape. Align the zipper tape with the edge of the fabric and center the zipper along that edge.

3. Sew ¼″ away from the edge. Press the pocket piece away from the zipper.

4. Place the zipper on top of a 8½″ × 5½″ pocket piece (*note the different size!*), right side of the fabric to the wrong side of the tape. Align the zipper tape with the edge of the fabric. The sides of both pocket pieces should line up with each other across the zipper. Sew ¼″ away from edge. Press the pocket piece away from the zipper.

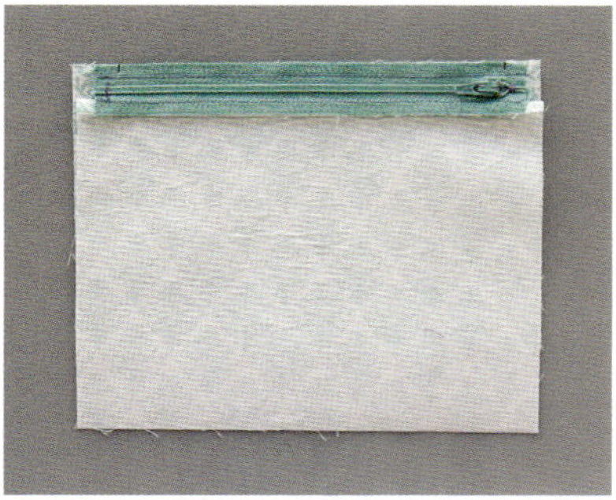

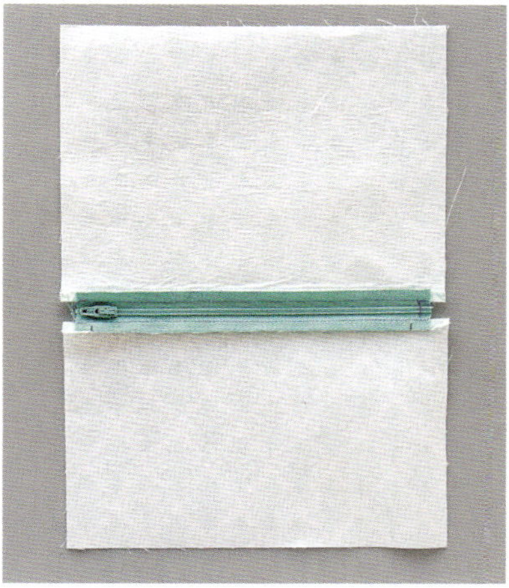

5. Repeat Steps 2–4 with the other zipper and pocket pieces. Set both zipper/pocket pieces aside.

6. Cut out the zipper pocket rectangle on the outside front piece. If you've woven your front, be careful not to pull on the stitches or dislodge a woven strip.

Note: If you'd like to ensure your edgestitching stays tidy, you can topstitch ⅛″ outside the cutting line before you cut out the zipper pocket rectangle. Make sure to use a longer-than-normal stitch. When you stitch the zipper in place in Step 8 (below), stitch on top of this line of stitches.

7. Center 1 outside zipper-with-pocket piece right side up underneath the cutout. The 6½″ pocket piece will be toward the top, and the 5½″ piece will be toward the bottom. Make sure the zipper pocket pieces are spread out and away from the zipper. I use a bit of glue under the edges of the zipper opening to hold the zipper in place.

8. Topstitch around the opening, ⅛″ away from the edge. Set aside.

9. To create the zipper pocket opening on the back lining piece, begin by preparing the frame. On the kraft•tex zipper-pocket frame, use chalk or a pencil to draw a rectangle ⅜″ in from each of the 4 edges. Cut out this rectangle.

10. On the lining back piece, cut out the solid line of the lining zipper-pocket placement lines.

11. Use the zipper-pocket frame marks on the lining to position the kraft•tex frame over the lining opening.

12. Feed the key-hook strap you set aside in Create the Straps, Step 3 (page 15) through the small swivel hook. Fold the strap in half, and pin or glue tack the loose ends under the kraft•tex frame, 1″ from an end. Pin or glue tack the frame in place.

13. Topstitch around the outside of the frame.

14. Repeat Steps 7 and 8 to sew in the lining zipper pocket.

15. To finish the front zipper pocket, turn the front right side down so that the pocket pieces are faceup. Fold the top pocket piece down over the bottom piece. Folding the front kraft•tex piece under and away from the edges of the pocket, use a ½″ seam to sew the 3 open sides of the pocket pieces together. *Note:* If your 2 pocket pieces do not line up on the bottom, that's fine. Trim the longer one to meet the shorter before stitching, if desired.

16. Repeat Step 15 to finish the lining zipper pocket.

Prepare the Top Zipper

If you are using a zipper longer than 12″, you will need to shorten the zipper (see Shortening a Zipper, below).

1. Trim the zipper tape ½″ away from the zipper start and stop so the zipper tape measures 13″ total.

SHORTENING A ZIPPER

This bag calls for one zipper 12″ long and two zippers 7″ long. If you are going to use a longer zipper, it is easy to shorten it!

1. Measure your zipper and mark the length called for. (For example, a 12″ zipper has 12″ of zipper tape total, including the opening stop and closing stop.) I prefer to include the zipper's opening stop when shortening a zipper.

2. Stitch across the zipper ¼″ outside the marked lines. If you are using a metal zipper, stitch up to the zipper teeth and then use the fly wheel to move the needle forward carefully, guiding it between the teeth to reach the other side. Pivot and stitch back carefully. If you are using a polyester zipper, you can safely zigzag stitch over the zipper teeth. If called for in the project, trim the extra zipper tape away from both ends of the zipper, ½″ away from the measured marks. The entire length of the zipper tape will now be 1″ longer than the zipper length called for in the project.

2. Fold a 2″ × 2″ zipper tab in half. Fold in one edge to meet at the center fold. Press.

Wrong side of zipper tab

3. Place the zipper right side up on top of the zipper tab right side up, aligning one end of the zipper tape with the unfolded edge of the zipper tab. Stitch with a ½″ seam, just outside of the zipper start or stop.

4. Fold the folded end of the zipper tab to the front of the zipper and topstitch along the edge.

5. Trim off the 2 sides even with the zipper tape.

6. Repeat Steps 2–5 with the other end of the zipper and the other tab.

Attach the Top Zipper

Before installing the top zipper, note the front zipper pocket. Does the zipper head rest to the right or left when closed? It's nice if the closed resting position of zipper head on the top matches the one on the pocket.

1. Place the zipper on top of the bag's outside front, right sides together. Align the top edge of the bag with the top edge of the zipper tape and center the tape along that edge. There should be ½″ on each end. Pin or glue tack along the edge.

2. Place the lining front, right side down, on top of the zipper/bag front. (The outside bag front and lining bag front will be right sides together, and the zipper will be sandwiched between them.) Pin or glue tack along the edge.

3. Using a zipper foot, stitch with a ¼″ seam. Start sewing farthest away from the zipper head. As you approach it, stop with the needle down in the fabric, lift the foot, and push the zipper head under the foot and out of the way. Finish stitching.

4. Press the outside and lining away from the zipper.

5. Topstitch along the edge.

6. Repeat Steps 1–5 for the bag backs on the other side of the zipper.

Construct the Bag

1. Open the zipper three-quarters of the way.

2. Open up and reorganize the pieces so that the 2 outside pieces are right sides together on one side of the zipper and the 2 lining pieces are rights sides together on the other. Carefully push or fold the zipper toward the lining side. (The key to a tidy zipper is to not catch the zipper tab in the side seam—but it helps if the zipper is folded neatly in one direction.)

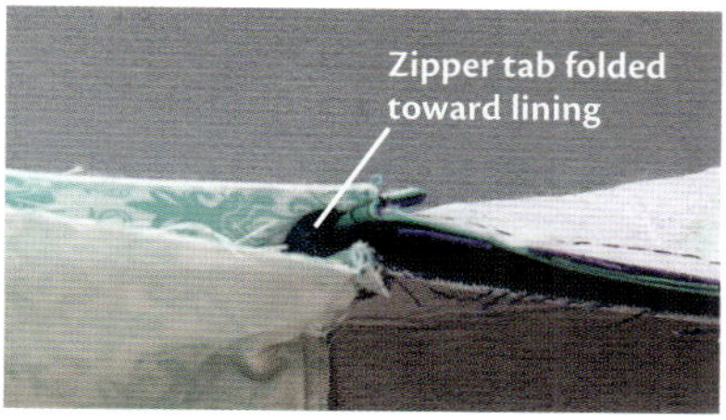

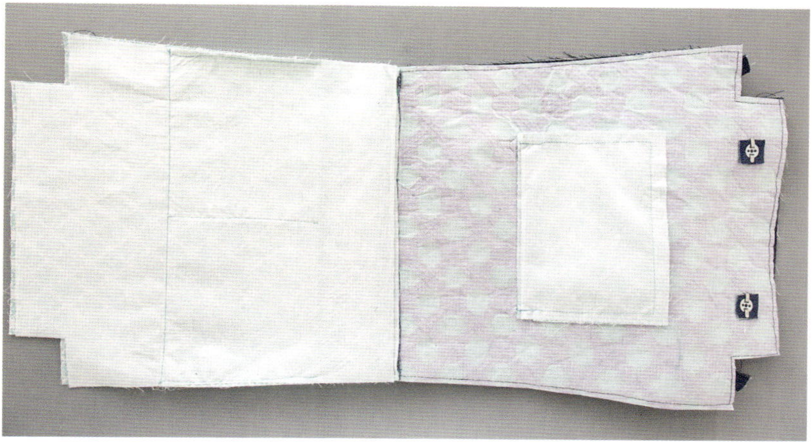

3. Pin or glue tack the side seams and bottom seams, leaving about a 9″ opening in one side of the linings.

4. Stitch the bottom seam together on both the outsides and the linings.

5. Sew the side seam without the opening: Start at the edge of the bag's bottom corner cutout on the outsides and end at the edge of the bag's bottom corner cutout on the linings, carefully avoiding the zipper tab along the way.

6. Sew the other side seam, backstitching on both sides of the large opening left in the lining for turning. Trim off the ends of the buckle straps.

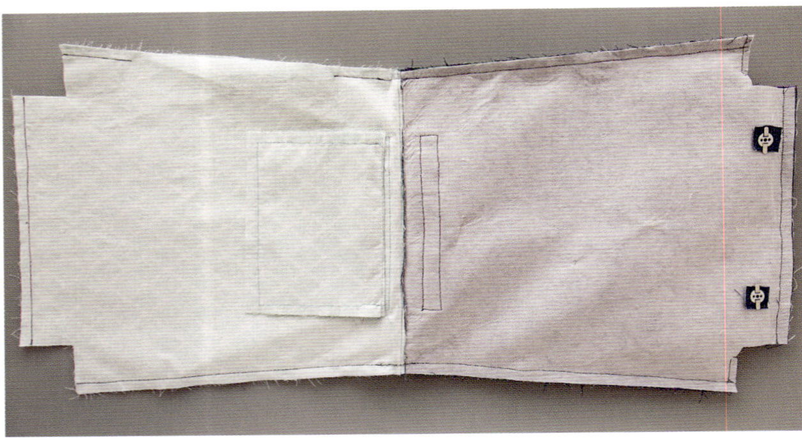

7. To box the bottom lining corners, fold the bottom of the lining so that the side seam matches up with the bottom seam and the bottom corner cutouts form a straight line. Stitch with a ½″ seam. ***Fig. A***

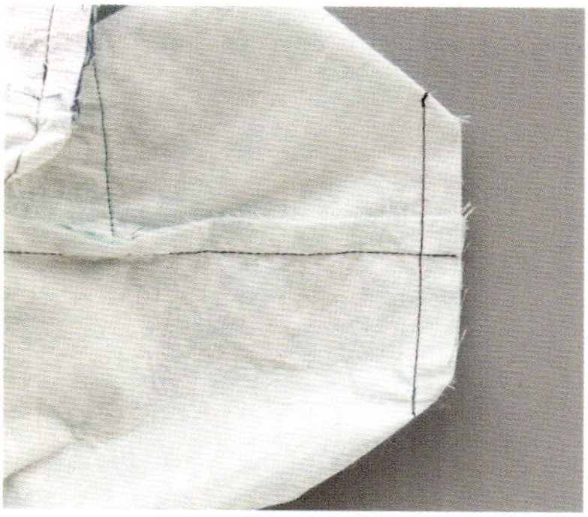

A

8. Repeat Step 7 with the other corner of the lining.

9. On the outside bag corners, you are going to box the corners and insert the base at the same time. Fold the bottom of the bag outside so that the side seam matches up with the bottom seam and the bottom corner cutouts form a straight line. Place the wrapped base on the bottom, with one end lined up with the bottom corner cutout. Stitch through the bag's bottom corner and base with a ½″ seam. ***Fig. B***

B

10. Repeat Step 9 with the other outside corner.

11. Turn the bag right side out through the lining. Topstitch the opening in the lining closed, and push the lining into the bag, poking out all of the corners.

Charlie kraft•tex Wristlet

Finished wristlet: 8″ wide × 4½″ high × 1¼″ deep

MATERIALS

kraft•tex 1: 6½″ × 7¾″ scrap

kraft•tex 2: 6″ × 11″ scrap

Front fabric (use only if not weaving with kraft•tex): 11″ × 5½″ scrap

Back fabric: ¼ yard

Lining fabric: ¼ yard

Fusible interfacing (stiff): ⅔ yard

7″ zipper: 1 for top

CUTTING

Front fabric

kraft•tex 1

- Cut 11 strips ½″ × 6½″ for weaving.
- Cut 10 strips 3⁄16″ × 6½″ for weaving.

kraft•tex 2

- Cut 1 strip ¾″ × 11″ for weaving.
- Cut 7 strips ½″ × 11″ for weaving.
- Cut 7 strips 3⁄16″ × 11″ for weaving.

Back fabric

- Cut 1 piece 11″ × 5½″ for the back.
- Cut 1 strip 2″ × 15″ for the strap.
- Cut 2 squares 2″ × 2″ for the zipper tabs.

Lining fabric

- Cut 2 pieces 11″ × 5½″ for the front and back lining.

Interfacing

- Cut 4 pieces 11″ × 5½″ for the fronts and backs.
- Cut 1 strip 2″ × 15″ for the strap. (Strap interfacing is not necessary if your fabric is heavy denim.)

Weaving

1. Edgestitch both sides of the ½″ kraft•tex 1 and 2 strips.

2. Use the weaving template to space apart the vertical kraft•tex 1 strips.

3. Tape the strips down along the top edge.

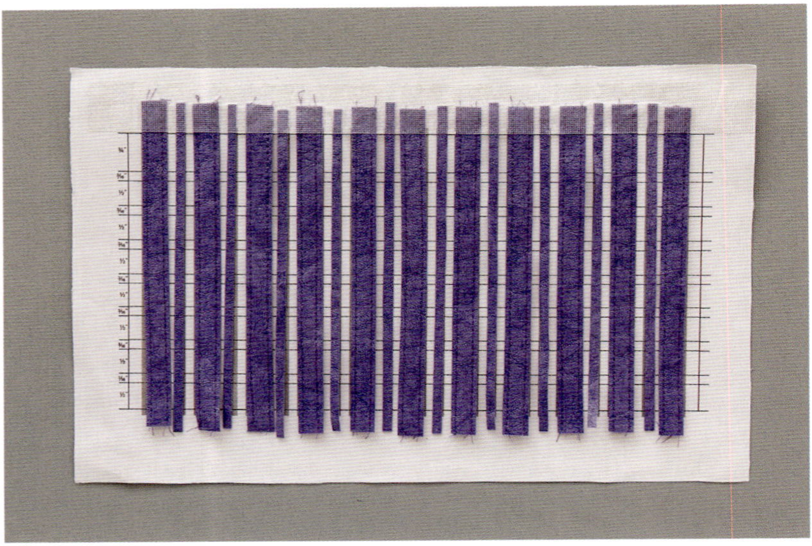

4. Weave in the horizontal kraft•tex 2 strips, starting with a ¾″ strip and then alternating 3⁄16″ strips and ½″ strips. As necessary in your weaving, snug the strips up tight to each other.

5. The last strip on the bottom will be a ½″ strip.

6. Fuse the interfacing on the back side of the woven panel, carefully centering on a vertical strip.

7. Place the Charlie kraft•tex Wristlet front and back pattern on top of the grid, and center on a vertical strip. Trace the pattern onto the prepared grid.

8. Stitch ⅛″ in from the marked cut line.

9. Cut out the front along the marked lines.

Prepare the Fronts and Backs

1. Fuse the interfacing to the outside back and the lining front and back pieces.

2. Use the front and back pattern to cut out the outside back and the lining front and back pieces.

Make the Strap

1. Fold the 2″ × 15″ strap in half along the length. Press. Reopen and fold both edges toward the middle to create a ½″ × 15″ strap.

2. Topstitch along the long edges.

3. Fold the strap in half. Position it on the outside back piece, 1″ down from the top, with the raw edges aligned and the folded strap pointing toward the center of the back. Baste in place ¼″ in from the edge.

Prepare the Zipper

- If you are using a zipper longer than 7″, see Shortening a Zipper (page 26).
- Follow Charlie kraft•tex Backpack, Prepare the Top Zipper, Steps 1–6 (page 26).
- In Step 1, trim your zipper tape to 8″ total.

Attach the Zipper

- Follow Charlie kraft•tex Backpack, Attach the Top Zipper, Steps 1–6 (pages 27 and 28).

Construct the Bag

- Follow Charlie kraft•tex Backpack, Construct the Bag, Steps 1–11 (pages 29–31).
- In Steps 3, 4, and 6, leave the opening in the bottom lining seam instead of the side seam.
- In Step 7, use a ¼″ seam.
- In Steps 9 and 10, there is no base to include in the outside corners. Use a ¼″ seam.

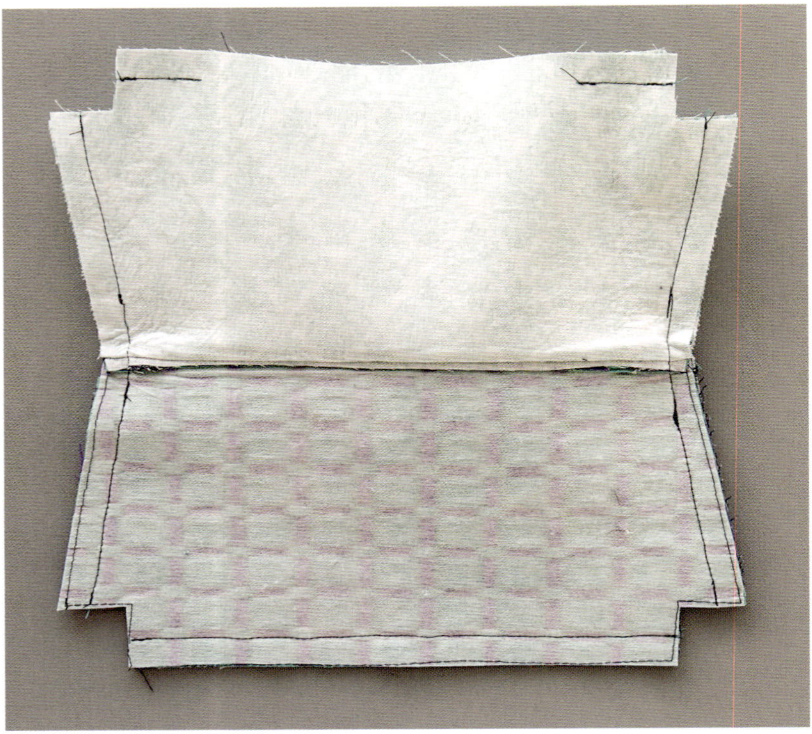